Fluency in Number Facts
Years 3 & 4

Peter Clarke

William Collins' dream of knowledge for all began with the publication of his first book in 1819. A self-educated mill worker, he not only enriched millions of lives, but also founded a flourishing publishing house. Today, staying true to this spirit, Collins books are packed with inspiration, innovation and practical expertise. They place you at the centre of a world of possibility and give you exactly what you need to explore it.

Collins. Freedom to teach.

Published by Collins

An imprint of HarperCollins*Publishers*
77–85 Fulham Palace Road
Hammersmith
London
W6 8JB

Browse the complete Collins catalogue at
www.collins.co.uk

10 9 8 7 6 5 4 3 2 1

ISBN-978-0-00-753131-8

British Library Cataloguing in Publication Data
A Catalogue record for this publication is available from the British Library

Edited by Gaynor Spry
Cover design by Nikki Kenwood
Cover artwork by Gwyneth Williams
Internal design by Nikki Kenwood
Illustrations by Ilias Arahovitis and Jouve
Typeset by Jouve

Printed by L.E.G.O. S.p.A. - Italy

Acknowledgement
The author wishes to thank Brian Molyneaux for his valuable contribution to this publication.

Contents

Addition and subtraction number facts to 20

Number facts for 0

$0 + 0 = 0$	$0 - 0 = 0$

Number facts for 1

$1 + 0 = 1$	$1 - 0 = 1$
$0 + 1 = 1$	$1 - 1 = 0$

Number facts for 2

$2 + 0 = 2$	$2 - 0 = 2$
$1 + 1 = 2$	$2 - 1 = 1$
$0 + 2 = 2$	$2 - 2 = 0$

Number facts for 3

$3 + 0 = 3$	$3 - 0 = 3$
$2 + 1 = 3$	$3 - 1 = 2$
$1 + 2 = 3$	$3 - 2 = 1$
$0 + 3 = 3$	$3 - 3 = 0$

Number facts for 4

$4 + 0 = 4$	$4 - 0 = 4$
$3 + 1 = 4$	$4 - 1 = 3$
$2 + 2 = 4$	$4 - 2 = 2$
$1 + 3 = 4$	$4 - 3 = 1$
$0 + 4 = 4$	$4 - 4 = 0$

Number facts for 5

$5 + 0 = 5$	$5 - 0 = 5$
$4 + 1 = 5$	$5 - 1 = 4$
$3 + 2 = 5$	$5 - 2 = 3$
$2 + 3 = 5$	$5 - 3 = 2$
$1 + 4 = 5$	$5 - 4 = 1$
$0 + 5 = 5$	$5 - 5 = 0$

Number facts for 6

$6 + 0 = 6$	$6 - 0 = 6$
$5 + 1 = 6$	$6 - 1 = 5$
$4 + 2 = 6$	$6 - 2 = 4$
$3 + 3 = 6$	$6 - 3 = 3$
$2 + 4 = 6$	$6 - 4 = 2$
$1 + 5 = 6$	$6 - 5 = 1$
$0 + 6 = 6$	$6 - 6 = 0$

Number facts for 7

$7 + 0 = 7$	$7 - 0 = 7$
$6 + 1 = 7$	$7 - 1 = 6$
$5 + 2 = 7$	$7 - 2 = 5$
$4 + 3 = 7$	$7 - 3 = 4$
$3 + 4 = 7$	$7 - 4 = 3$
$2 + 5 = 7$	$7 - 5 = 2$
$1 + 6 = 7$	$7 - 6 = 1$
$0 + 7 = 7$	$7 - 7 = 0$

Number facts for 8

$8 + 0 = 8$	$8 - 0 = 8$
$7 + 1 = 8$	$8 - 1 = 7$
$6 + 2 = 8$	$8 - 2 = 6$
$5 + 3 = 8$	$8 - 3 = 5$
$4 + 4 = 8$	$8 - 4 = 4$
$3 + 5 = 8$	$8 - 5 = 3$
$2 + 6 = 8$	$8 - 6 = 2$
$1 + 7 = 8$	$8 - 7 = 1$
$0 + 8 = 8$	$8 - 8 = 0$

Number facts for 9

$9 + 0 = 9$	$9 - 0 = 9$
$8 + 1 = 9$	$9 - 1 = 8$
$7 + 2 = 9$	$9 - 2 = 7$
$6 + 3 = 9$	$9 - 3 = 6$
$5 + 4 = 9$	$9 - 4 = 5$
$4 + 5 = 9$	$9 - 5 = 4$
$3 + 6 = 9$	$9 - 6 = 3$
$2 + 7 = 9$	$9 - 7 = 2$
$1 + 8 = 9$	$9 - 8 = 1$
$0 + 9 = 9$	$9 - 9 = 0$

Number facts for 10

$10 + 0 = 10$	$10 - 0 = 10$
$9 + 1 = 10$	$10 - 1 = 9$
$8 + 2 = 10$	$10 - 2 = 8$
$7 + 3 = 10$	$10 - 3 = 7$
$6 + 4 = 10$	$10 - 4 = 6$
$5 + 5 = 10$	$10 - 5 = 5$
$4 + 6 = 10$	$10 - 6 = 4$
$3 + 7 = 10$	$10 - 7 = 3$
$2 + 8 = 10$	$10 - 8 = 2$
$1 + 9 = 10$	$10 - 9 = 1$
$0 + 10 = 10$	$10 - 10 = 0$

Number facts for 11

$11 + 0 = 11$	$11 - 0 = 11$
$10 + 1 = 11$	$11 - 1 = 10$
$9 + 2 = 11$	$11 - 2 = 9$
$8 + 3 = 11$	$11 - 3 = 8$
$7 + 4 = 11$	$11 - 4 = 7$
$6 + 5 = 11$	$11 - 5 = 6$
$5 + 6 = 11$	$11 - 6 = 5$
$4 + 7 = 11$	$11 - 7 = 4$
$3 + 8 = 11$	$11 - 8 = 3$
$2 + 9 = 11$	$11 - 9 = 2$
$1 + 10 = 11$	$11 - 10 = 1$
$0 + 11 = 11$	$11 - 11 = 0$

Number facts for 12

12 + 0 = 12	12 − 0 = 12
11 + 1 = 12	12 − 1 = 11
10 + 2 = 12	12 − 2 = 10
9 + 3 = 12	12 − 3 = 9
8 + 4 = 12	12 − 4 = 8
7 + 5 = 12	12 − 5 = 7
6 + 6 = 12	12 − 6 = 6
5 + 7 = 12	12 − 7 = 5
4 + 8 = 12	12 − 8 = 4
3 + 9 = 12	12 − 9 = 3
2 + 10 = 12	12 − 10 = 2
1 + 11 = 12	12 − 11 = 1
0 + 12 = 12	12 − 12 = 0

Number facts for 13

13 + 0 = 13	13 − 0 = 13
12 + 1 = 13	13 − 1 = 12
11 + 2 = 13	13 − 2 = 11
10 + 3 = 13	13 − 3 = 10
9 + 4 = 13	13 − 4 = 9
8 + 5 = 13	13 − 5 = 8
7 + 6 = 13	13 − 6 = 7
6 + 7 = 13	13 − 7 = 6
5 + 8 = 13	13 − 8 = 5
4 + 9 = 13	13 − 9 = 4
3 + 10 = 13	13 − 10 = 3
2 + 11 = 13	13 − 11 = 2
1 + 12 = 13	13 − 12 = 1
0 + 13 = 13	13 − 13 = 0

Number facts for 14

14 + 0 = 14	14 − 0 = 14
13 + 1 = 14	14 − 1 = 13
12 + 2 = 14	14 − 2 = 12
11 + 3 = 14	14 − 3 = 11
10 + 4 = 14	14 − 4 = 10
9 + 5 = 14	14 − 5 = 9
8 + 6 = 14	14 − 6 = 8
7 + 7 = 14	14 − 7 = 7
6 + 8 = 14	14 − 8 = 6
5 + 9 = 14	14 − 9 = 5
4 + 10 = 14	14 − 10 = 4
3 + 11 = 14	14 − 11 = 3
2 + 12 = 14	14 − 12 = 2
1 + 13 = 14	14 − 13 = 1
0 + 14 = 14	14 − 14 = 0

Number facts for 15

15 + 0 = 15	15 − 0 = 15
14 + 1 = 15	15 − 1 = 14
13 + 2 = 15	15 − 2 = 13
12 + 3 = 15	15 − 3 = 12
11 + 4 = 15	15 − 4 = 11
10 + 5 = 15	15 − 5 = 10
9 + 6 = 15	15 − 6 = 9
8 + 7 = 15	15 − 7 = 8
7 + 8 = 15	15 − 8 = 7
6 + 9 = 15	15 − 9 = 6
5 + 10 = 15	15 − 10 = 5
4 + 11 = 15	15 − 11 = 4
3 + 12 = 15	15 − 12 = 3
2 + 13 = 15	15 − 13 = 2
1 + 14 = 15	15 − 14 = 1
0 + 15 = 15	15 − 15 = 0

Number facts for 16

16 + 0 = 16	16 − 0 = 16
15 + 1 = 16	16 − 1 = 15
14 + 2 = 16	16 − 2 = 14
13 + 3 = 16	16 − 3 = 13
12 + 4 = 16	16 − 4 = 12
11 + 5 = 16	16 − 5 = 11
10 + 6 = 16	16 − 6 = 10
9 + 7 = 16	16 − 7 = 9
8 + 8 = 16	16 − 8 = 8
7 + 9 = 16	16 − 9 = 7
6 + 10 = 16	16 − 10 = 6
5 + 11 = 16	16 − 11 = 5
4 + 12 = 16	16 − 12 = 4
3 + 13 = 16	16 − 13 = 3
2 + 14 = 16	16 − 14 = 2
1 + 15 = 16	16 − 15 = 1
0 + 16 = 16	16 − 16 = 0

Number facts for 17

17 + 0 = 17	17 − 0 = 17
16 + 1 = 17	17 − 1 = 16
15 + 2 = 17	17 − 2 = 15
14 + 3 = 17	17 − 3 = 14
13 + 4 = 17	17 − 4 = 13
12 + 5 = 17	17 − 5 = 12
11 + 6 = 17	17 − 6 = 11
10 + 7 = 17	17 − 7 = 10
9 + 8 = 17	17 − 8 = 9
8 + 9 = 17	17 − 9 = 8
7 + 10 = 17	17 − 10 = 7
6 + 11 = 17	17 − 11 = 6
5 + 12 = 17	17 − 12 = 5
4 + 13 = 17	17 − 13 = 4
3 + 14 = 17	17 − 14 = 3
2 + 15 = 17	17 − 15 = 2
1 + 16 = 17	17 − 16 = 1
0 + 17 = 17	17 − 17 = 0

Number facts for 18

18 + 0 = 18	18 − 0 = 18
17 + 1 = 18	18 − 1 = 17
16 + 2 = 18	18 − 2 = 16
15 + 3 = 18	18 − 3 = 15
14 + 4 = 18	18 − 4 = 14
13 + 5 = 18	18 − 5 = 13
12 + 6 = 18	18 − 6 = 12
11 + 7 = 18	18 − 7 = 11
10 + 8 = 18	18 − 8 = 10
9 + 9 = 18	18 − 9 = 9
8 + 10 = 18	18 − 10 = 8
7 + 11 = 18	18 − 11 = 7
6 + 12 = 18	18 − 12 = 6
5 + 13 = 18	18 − 13 = 5
4 + 14 = 18	18 − 14 = 4
3 + 15 = 18	18 − 15 = 3
2 + 16 = 18	18 − 16 = 2
1 + 17 = 18	18 − 17 = 1
0 + 18 = 18	18 − 18 = 0

Number facts for 19

19 + 0 = 19	19 − 0 = 19
18 + 1 = 19	19 − 1 = 18
17 + 2 = 19	19 − 2 = 17
16 + 3 = 19	19 − 3 = 16
15 + 4 = 19	19 − 4 = 15
14 + 5 = 19	19 − 5 = 14
13 + 6 = 19	19 − 6 = 13
12 + 7 = 19	19 − 7 = 12
11 + 8 = 19	19 − 8 = 11
10 + 9 = 19	19 − 9 = 10
9 + 10 = 19	19 − 10 = 9
8 + 11 = 19	19 − 11 = 8
7 + 12 = 19	19 − 12 = 7
6 + 13 = 19	19 − 13 = 6
5 + 14 = 19	19 − 14 = 5
4 + 15 = 19	19 − 15 = 4
3 + 16 = 19	19 − 16 = 3
2 + 17 = 19	19 − 17 = 2
1 + 18 = 19	19 − 18 = 1
0 + 19 = 19	19 − 19 = 0

Number facts for 20

20 + 0 = 20	20 − 0 = 20
19 + 1 = 20	20 − 1 = 19
18 + 2 = 20	20 − 2 = 18
17 + 3 = 20	20 − 3 = 17
16 + 4 = 20	20 − 4 = 16
15 + 5 = 20	20 − 5 = 15
14 + 6 = 20	20 − 6 = 14
13 + 7 = 20	20 − 7 = 13
12 + 8 = 20	20 − 8 = 12
11 + 9 = 20	20 − 9 = 11
10 + 10 = 20	20 − 10 = 10
9 + 11 = 20	20 − 11 = 9
8 + 12 = 20	20 − 12 = 8
7 + 13 = 20	20 − 13 = 7
6 + 14 = 20	20 − 14 = 6
5 + 15 = 20	20 − 15 = 5
4 + 16 = 20	20 − 16 = 4
3 + 17 = 20	20 − 17 = 3
2 + 18 = 20	20 − 18 = 2
1 + 19 = 20	20 − 19 = 1
0 + 20 = 20	20 − 20 = 0

Addition and subtraction trios to 20

Trios for 2

2 + 0 = 2
0 + 2 = 2
2 − 0 = 2
2 − 2 = 0

1 + 1 = 2
2 − 1 = 1

Trios for 3

3 + 0 = 3
0 + 3 = 3
3 − 0 = 3
3 − 3 = 0

2 + 1 = 3
1 + 2 = 3
3 − 1 = 2
3 − 2 = 1

Trios for 4

4 + 0 = 4
0 + 4 = 4
4 − 0 = 4
4 − 4 = 0

3 + 1 = 4
1 + 3 = 4
4 − 1 = 3
4 − 3 = 1

2 + 2 = 4
4 − 2 = 2

Trios for 5

5 + 0 = 5
0 + 5 = 5
5 − 0 = 5
5 − 5 = 0

4 + 1 = 5
1 + 4 = 5
5 − 1 = 4
5 − 4 = 1

3 + 2 = 5
2 + 3 = 5
5 − 2 = 3
5 − 3 = 2

Trios for 6

6 + 0 = 6
0 + 6 = 6
6 − 0 = 6
6 − 6 = 0

5 + 1 = 6
1 + 5 = 6
6 − 1 = 5
6 − 5 = 1

4 + 2 = 6
2 + 4 = 6
6 − 2 = 4
6 − 4 = 2

3 + 3 = 6
6 − 3 = 3

Trios for 7

$7 + 0 = 7$	
$0 + 7 = 7$	
$7 - 0 = 7$	
$7 - 7 = 0$	

$6 + 1 = 7$
$1 + 6 = 7$
$7 - 1 = 6$
$7 - 6 = 1$

$5 + 2 = 7$
$2 + 5 = 7$
$7 - 2 = 5$
$7 - 5 = 2$

$4 + 3 = 7$
$3 + 4 = 7$
$7 - 3 = 4$
$7 - 4 = 3$

Trios for 8

$8 + 0 = 8$
$0 + 8 = 8$
$8 - 0 = 8$
$8 - 8 = 0$

$7 + 1 = 8$
$1 + 7 = 8$
$8 - 1 = 7$
$8 - 7 = 1$

$6 + 2 = 8$
$2 + 6 = 8$
$8 - 2 = 6$
$8 - 6 = 2$

$5 + 3 = 8$
$3 + 5 = 8$
$8 - 3 = 5$
$8 - 5 = 3$

$4 + 4 = 8$
$8 - 4 = 4$

Trios for 9

$9 + 0 = 9$
$0 + 9 = 9$
$9 - 0 = 9$
$9 - 9 = 0$

$8 + 1 = 9$
$1 + 8 = 9$
$9 - 1 = 8$
$9 - 8 = 1$

$7 + 2 = 9$
$2 + 7 = 9$
$9 - 2 = 7$
$9 - 7 = 2$

$6 + 3 = 9$
$3 + 6 = 9$
$9 - 3 = 6$
$9 - 6 = 3$

$5 + 4 = 9$
$4 + 5 = 9$
$9 - 4 = 5$
$9 - 5 = 4$

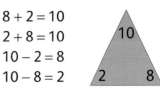

Trios for 10

10 + 0 = 10
0 + 10 = 10
10 − 0 = 10
10 − 10 = 0

9 + 1 = 10
1 + 9 = 10
10 − 1 = 9
10 − 9 = 1

8 + 2 = 10
2 + 8 = 10
10 − 2 = 8
10 − 8 = 2

7 + 3 = 10
3 + 7 = 10
10 − 3 = 7
10 − 7 = 3

6 + 4 = 10
4 + 6 = 10
10 − 4 = 6
10 − 6 = 4

5 + 5 = 10
10 − 5 = 5

Trios for 11

11 + 0 = 11
0 + 11 = 11
11 − 0 = 11
11 − 11 = 0

10 + 1 = 11
1 + 10 = 11
11 − 1 = 10
11 − 10 = 1

9 + 2 = 11
2 + 9 = 11
11 − 2 = 9
11 − 9 = 2

8 + 3 = 11
3 + 8 = 11
11 − 3 = 8
11 − 8 = 3

7 + 4 = 11
4 + 7 = 11
11 − 4 = 7
11 − 7 = 4

6 + 5 = 11
5 + 6 = 11
11 − 5 = 6
11 − 6 = 5

Trios for 12

12 + 0 = 12
0 + 12 = 12
12 − 0 = 12
12 − 12 = 0

11 + 1 = 12
1 + 11 = 12
12 − 1 = 11
12 − 11 = 1

10 + 2 = 12
2 + 10 = 12
12 − 2 = 10
12 − 10 = 2

9 + 3 = 12
3 + 9 = 12
12 − 3 = 9
12 − 9 = 3

8 + 4 = 12
4 + 8 = 12
12 − 4 = 8
12 − 8 = 4

7 + 5 = 12
5 + 7 = 12
12 − 5 = 7
12 − 7 = 5

6 + 6 = 12
12 − 6 = 6

Trios for 13

13 + 0 = 13
0 + 13 = 13
13 − 0 = 13
13 − 13 = 0

12 + 1 = 13
1 + 12 = 13
13 − 1 = 12
13 − 12 = 1

11 + 2 = 13
2 + 11 = 13
13 − 2 = 11
13 − 11 = 2

10 + 3 = 13
3 + 10 = 13
13 − 3 = 10
13 − 10 = 3

9 + 4 = 13
4 + 9 = 13
13 − 4 = 9
13 − 9 = 4

8 + 5 = 13
5 + 8 = 13
13 − 5 = 8
13 − 8 = 5

7 + 6 = 13
6 + 7 = 13
13 − 6 = 7
13 − 7 = 6

Trios for 14

14 + 0 = 14
0 + 14 = 14
14 − 0 = 14
14 − 14 = 0

13 + 1 = 14
1 + 13 = 14
14 − 1 = 13
14 − 13 = 1

12 + 2 = 14
2 + 12 = 14
14 − 2 = 12
14 − 12 = 2

11 + 3 = 14
3 + 11 = 14
14 − 3 = 11
14 − 11 = 3

10 + 4 = 14
4 + 10 = 14
14 − 4 = 10
14 − 10 = 4

9 + 5 = 14
5 + 9 = 14
14 − 5 = 9
14 − 9 = 5

8 + 6 = 14
6 + 8 = 14
14 − 6 = 8
14 − 8 = 6

7 + 7 = 14
14 − 7 = 7

Trios for 15

15 + 0 = 15
0 + 15 = 15
15 − 0 = 15
15 − 15 = 0

14 + 1 = 15
1 + 14 = 15
15 − 1 = 14
15 − 14 = 1

13 + 2 = 15
2 + 13 = 15
15 − 2 = 13
15 − 13 = 2

12 + 3 = 15
3 + 12 = 15
15 − 3 = 12
15 − 12 = 3

11 + 4 = 15
4 + 11 = 15
15 − 4 = 11
15 − 11 = 4

10 + 5 = 15
5 + 10 = 15
15 − 5 = 10
15 − 10 = 5

9 + 6 = 15
6 + 9 = 15
15 − 6 = 9
15 − 9 = 6

8 + 7 = 15
7 + 8 = 15
15 − 7 = 8
15 − 8 = 7

Trios for 16

16 + 0 = 16
0 + 16 = 16
16 − 0 = 16
16 − 16 = 0

15 + 1 = 16
1 + 15 = 16
16 − 1 = 15
16 − 15 = 1

14 + 2 = 16
2 + 14 = 16
16 − 2 = 14
16 − 14 = 2

13 + 3 = 16
3 + 13 = 16
16 − 3 = 13
16 − 13 = 3

12 + 4 = 16
4 + 12 = 16
16 − 4 = 12
16 − 12 = 4

11 + 5 = 16
5 + 11 = 16
16 − 5 = 11
16 − 11 = 5

10 + 6 = 16
6 + 10 = 16
16 − 6 = 10
16 − 10 = 6

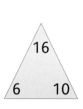

9 + 7 = 16
7 + 9 = 16
16 − 7 = 9
16 − 9 = 7

8 + 8 = 16
16 − 8 = 8

Trios for 17

$17 + 0 = 17$			
$0 + 17 = 17$			
$17 - 0 = 17$			
$17 - 17 = 0$			

17 / 0 / 17

$16 + 1 = 17$
$1 + 16 = 17$
$17 - 1 = 16$
$17 - 16 = 1$

17 / 1 / 16

$15 + 2 = 17$
$2 + 15 = 17$
$17 - 2 = 15$
$17 - 15 = 2$

17 / 2 / 15

$14 + 3 = 17$
$3 + 14 = 17$
$17 - 3 = 14$
$17 - 14 = 3$

17 / 3 / 14

$13 + 4 = 17$
$4 + 13 = 17$
$17 - 4 = 13$
$17 - 13 = 4$

17 / 4 / 13

$12 + 5 = 17$
$5 + 12 = 17$
$17 - 5 = 12$
$17 - 12 = 5$

17 / 5 / 12

$11 + 6 = 17$
$6 + 11 = 17$
$17 - 6 = 11$
$17 - 11 = 6$

17 / 6 / 11

$10 + 7 = 17$
$7 + 10 = 17$
$17 - 7 = 10$
$17 - 10 = 7$

17 / 7 / 10

$9 + 8 = 17$
$8 + 9 = 17$
$17 - 8 = 9$
$17 - 9 = 8$

17 / 8 / 9

Trios for 18

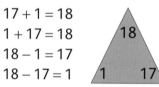

$18 + 0 = 18$
$0 + 18 = 18$
$18 - 0 = 18$
$18 - 18 = 0$

18 / 0 / 18

$17 + 1 = 18$
$1 + 17 = 18$
$18 - 1 = 17$
$18 - 17 = 1$

18 / 1 / 17

$16 + 2 = 18$
$2 + 16 = 18$
$18 - 2 = 16$
$18 - 16 = 2$

18 / 2 / 16

$15 + 3 = 18$
$3 + 15 = 18$
$18 - 3 = 15$
$18 - 15 = 3$

18 / 3 / 15

$14 + 4 = 18$
$4 + 14 = 18$
$18 - 4 = 14$
$18 - 14 = 4$

18 / 4 / 14

$13 + 5 = 18$
$5 + 13 = 18$
$18 - 5 = 13$
$18 - 13 = 5$

18 / 5 / 13

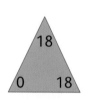

$12 + 6 = 18$
$6 + 12 = 18$
$18 - 6 = 12$
$18 - 12 = 6$

18 / 6 / 12

$11 + 7 = 18$
$7 + 11 = 18$
$18 - 7 = 11$
$18 - 11 = 7$

18 / 7 / 11

$10 + 8 = 18$
$8 + 10 = 18$
$18 - 8 = 10$
$18 - 10 = 8$

18 / 8 / 10

$9 + 9 = 18$
$18 - 9 = 9$

18 / 9 / 9

Trios for 19

$19 + 0 = 19$
$0 + 19 = 19$
$19 - 0 = 19$
$19 - 19 = 0$

19 / 0 / 19

$18 + 1 = 19$
$1 + 18 = 19$
$19 - 1 = 18$
$19 - 18 = 1$

19 / 1 / 18

$17 + 2 = 19$
$2 + 17 = 19$
$19 - 2 = 17$
$19 - 17 = 2$

19 / 2 / 17

$16 + 3 = 19$
$3 + 16 = 19$
$19 - 3 = 16$
$19 - 16 = 3$

19 / 3 / 16

$15 + 4 = 19$
$4 + 15 = 19$
$19 - 4 = 15$
$19 - 15 = 4$

19 / 4 / 15

$14 + 5 = 19$
$5 + 14 = 19$
$19 - 5 = 14$
$19 - 14 = 5$

19 / 5 / 14

$13 + 6 = 19$
$6 + 13 = 19$
$19 - 6 = 13$
$19 - 13 = 6$

19 / 6 / 13

$12 + 7 = 19$
$7 + 12 = 19$
$19 - 7 = 12$
$19 - 12 = 7$

19 / 7 / 12

$11 + 8 = 19$
$8 + 11 = 19$
$19 - 8 = 11$
$19 - 11 = 8$

19 / 8 / 11

$10 + 9 = 19$
$9 + 10 = 19$
$19 - 9 = 10$
$19 - 10 = 9$

19 / 9 / 10

Trios for 20

$20 + 0 = 20$
$0 + 20 = 20$
$20 - 0 = 20$
$20 - 20 = 0$

20 / 0 / 20

$19 + 1 = 20$
$1 + 19 = 20$
$20 - 1 = 19$
$20 - 19 = 1$

20 / 1 / 19

$18 + 2 = 20$
$2 + 18 = 20$
$20 - 2 = 18$
$20 - 18 = 2$

20 / 2 / 18

$17 + 3 = 20$
$3 + 17 = 20$
$20 - 3 = 17$
$20 - 17 = 3$

20 / 3 / 17

$16 + 4 = 20$
$4 + 16 = 20$
$20 - 4 = 16$
$20 - 16 = 4$

20 / 4 / 16

$15 + 5 = 20$
$5 + 15 = 20$
$20 - 5 = 15$
$20 - 15 = 5$

20 / 5 / 15

$14 + 6 = 20$
$6 + 14 = 20$
$20 - 6 = 14$
$20 - 14 = 6$

20 / 6 / 14

$13 + 7 = 20$
$7 + 13 = 20$
$20 - 7 = 13$
$20 - 13 = 7$

20 / 7 / 13

$12 + 8 = 20$
$8 + 12 = 20$
$20 - 8 = 12$
$20 - 12 = 8$

20 / 8 / 12

$11 + 9 = 20$
$9 + 11 = 20$
$20 - 9 = 11$
$20 - 11 = 9$

20 / 9 / 11

$10 + 10 = 20$
$20 - 10 = 10$

20 / 10 / 10

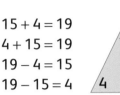
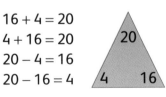
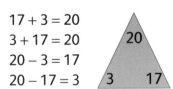
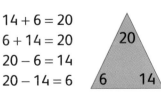

Addition number facts to **10** and **20** table

Addition can be done in any order.

So, $2 + 3 = 5$ and $3 + 2 = 5$

Addition is the opposite of subtraction.

So, if you know that $3 + 2 = 5$ you also know that:

$5 - 3 = 2$ and $5 - 2 = 3$

+	0	1	2	3	4	5	6	7	8	9	10
0	0	1	2	3	4	5	6	7	8	9	10
1	1	2	3	4	5	6	7	8	9	10	11
2	2	3	4	5	6	7	8	9	10	11	12
3	3	4	5	6	7	8	9	10	11	12	13
4	4	5	6	7	8	9	10	11	12	13	14
5	5	6	7	8	9	10	11	12	13	14	15
6	6	7	8	9	10	11	12	13	14	15	16
7	7	8	9	10	11	12	13	14	15	16	17
8	8	9	10	11	12	13	14	15	16	17	18
9	9	10	11	12	13	14	15	16	17	18	19
10	10	11	12	13	14	15	16	17	18	19	20

Addition of 1-digit and 2-digit numbers to 20 table

+	11	12	13	14	15	16	17	18	19	20
0	11	12	13	14	15	16	17	18	19	20
1	12	13	14	15	16	17	18	19	20	
2	13	14	15	16	17	18	19	20		
3	14	15	16	17	18	19	20			
4	15	16	17	18	19	20				
5	16	17	18	19	20					
6	17	18	19	20						
7	18	19	20							
8	19	20								
9	20									

Multiples of 10 addition and subtraction table

If you know that $6 + 8 = 14$, then you can use this to work out facts such as:

$60 + 80 = 140$

$600 + 800 = 1400$

Addition can be done in any order.

So, $60 + 80 = 140$

and $80 + 60 = 140$

Addition is the inverse of subtraction. So, if you know that $60 + 80 = 140$ you also know that:

$140 - 60 = 80$

$140 - 80 = 60$

+	0	10	20	30	40	50	60	70	80	90	100
0	0	10	20	30	40	50	60	70	80	90	100
10	10	20	30	40	50	60	70	80	90	100	110
20	20	30	40	50	60	70	80	90	100	110	120
30	30	40	50	60	70	80	90	100	110	120	130
40	40	50	60	70	80	90	100	110	120	130	140
50	50	60	70	80	90	100	110	120	130	140	150
60	60	70	80	90	100	110	120	130	140	150	160
70	70	80	90	100	110	120	130	140	150	160	170
80	80	90	100	110	120	130	140	150	160	170	180
90	90	100	110	120	130	140	150	160	170	180	190
100	100	110	120	130	140	150	160	170	180	190	200

If you know that $14 + 3 = 17$, then you can use this to work out facts such as:

$140 + 30 = 170$

Addition can be done in any order.

So, $140 + 30 = 170$

and $30 + 140 = 170$

Addition is the inverse of subtraction. So, if you know that $140 + 30 = 170$ you also know that:

$170 - 30 = 140$

$170 - 140 = 30$

+	110	120	130	140	150	160	170	180	190	200
0	110	120	130	140	150	160	170	180	190	200
10	120	130	140	150	160	170	180	190	200	210
20	130	140	150	160	170	180	190	200	210	220
30	140	150	160	170	180	190	200	210	220	230
40	150	160	170	180	190	200	210	220	230	240
50	160	170	180	190	200	210	220	230	240	250
60	170	180	190	200	210	220	230	240	250	260
70	180	190	200	210	220	230	240	250	260	270
80	190	200	210	220	230	240	250	260	270	280
90	200	210	220	230	240	250	260	270	280	290
100	210	220	230	240	250	260	270	280	290	300

Multiplication tables to 12 × 12

2 times table

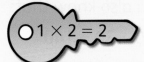 1 × 2 = 2

2 × 2 = 4

3 × 2 = 6

4 × 2 = 8

5 × 2 = 10

6 × 2 = 12

7 × 2 = 14

8 × 2 = 16

9 × 2 = 18

10 × 2 = 20

11 × 2 = 22

12 × 2 = 24

4 times table

 1 × 4 = 4

2 × 4 = 8

3 × 4 = 12

4 × 4 = 16

5 × 4 = 20

6 × 4 = 24

7 × 4 = 28

8 × 4 = 32

9 × 4 = 36

10 × 4 = 40

11 × 4 = 44

12 × 4 = 48

8 times table

 1 × 8 = 8

2 × 8 = 16

3 × 8 = 24

4 × 8 = 32

5 × 8 = 40

6 × 8 = 48

7 × 8 = 56

8 × 8 = 64

9 × 8 = 72

10 × 8 = 80

11 × 8 = 88

12 × 8 = 96

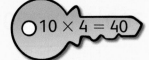
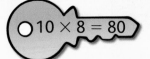

3 times table	6 times table	12 times table

 $1 \times 3 = 3$

 $1 \times 6 = 6$

 $1 \times 12 = 12$

$2 \times 3 = 6$ $2 \times 6 = 12$ $2 \times 12 = 24$

$3 \times 3 = 9$ $3 \times 6 = 18$ $3 \times 12 = 36$

$4 \times 3 = 12$ $4 \times 6 = 24$ $4 \times 12 = 48$

 $5 \times 3 = 15$

 $5 \times 6 = 30$

 $5 \times 12 = 60$

$6 \times 3 = 18$ $6 \times 6 = 36$ $6 \times 12 = 72$

$7 \times 3 = 21$ $7 \times 6 = 42$ $7 \times 12 = 84$

$8 \times 3 = 24$ $8 \times 6 = 48$ $8 \times 12 = 96$

$9 \times 3 = 27$ $9 \times 6 = 54$ $9 \times 12 = 108$

 $10 \times 3 = 30$

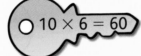 $10 \times 6 = 60$

 $10 \times 12 = 120$

$11 \times 3 = 33$ $11 \times 6 = 66$ $11 \times 12 = 132$

$12 \times 3 = 36$ $12 \times 6 = 72$ $12 \times 12 = 144$

5 times table	10 times table
 $1 \times 5 = 5$	 $1 \times 10 = 10$
 $2 \times 5 = 10$	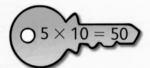 $2 \times 10 = 20$
$3 \times 5 = 15$	$3 \times 10 = 30$
$4 \times 5 = 20$	$4 \times 10 = 40$
 $5 \times 5 = 25$	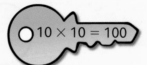 $5 \times 10 = 50$
$6 \times 5 = 30$	$6 \times 10 = 60$
$7 \times 5 = 35$	$7 \times 10 = 70$
$8 \times 5 = 40$	$8 \times 10 = 80$
$9 \times 5 = 45$	$9 \times 10 = 90$
$10 \times 5 = 50$	$10 \times 10 = 100$
$11 \times 5 = 55$	$11 \times 10 = 110$
$12 \times 5 = 60$	$12 \times 10 = 120$

7 times table

$3 \times 7 = 21$
$4 \times 7 = 28$

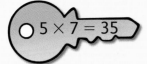

$6 \times 7 = 42$
$7 \times 7 = 49$
$8 \times 7 = 56$
$9 \times 7 = 63$

$11 \times 7 = 77$
$12 \times 7 = 84$

9 times table

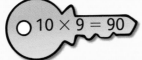

$3 \times 9 = 27$
$4 \times 9 = 36$

$6 \times 9 = 54$
$7 \times 9 = 63$
$8 \times 9 = 72$
$9 \times 9 = 81$

$11 \times 9 = 99$
$12 \times 9 = 108$

11 times table

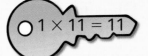

$3 \times 11 = 33$
$4 \times 11 = 44$

$6 \times 11 = 66$
$7 \times 11 = 77$
$8 \times 11 = 88$
$9 \times 11 = 99$

$11 \times 11 = 121$
$12 \times 11 = 132$

Division facts relating to the multiplication tables to 12 × 12

Division facts related to the 2 times table	**Division facts related to the 4 times table**	**Division facts related to the 8 times table**
$2 \div 2 = 1$	$4 \div 4 = 1$	$8 \div 8 = 1$
$4 \div 2 = 2$	$8 \div 4 = 2$	$16 \div 8 = 2$
$6 \div 2 = 3$	$12 \div 4 = 3$	$24 \div 8 = 3$
$8 \div 2 = 4$	$16 \div 4 = 4$	$32 \div 8 = 4$
$10 \div 2 = 5$	$20 \div 4 = 5$	$40 \div 8 = 5$
$12 \div 2 = 6$	$24 \div 4 = 6$	$48 \div 8 = 6$
$14 \div 2 = 7$	$28 \div 4 = 7$	$56 \div 8 = 7$
$16 \div 2 = 8$	$32 \div 4 = 8$	$64 \div 8 = 8$
$18 \div 2 = 9$	$36 \div 4 = 9$	$72 \div 8 = 9$
$20 \div 2 = 10$	$40 \div 4 = 10$	$80 \div 8 = 10$
$22 \div 2 = 11$	$44 \div 4 = 11$	$88 \div 8 = 11$
$24 \div 2 = 12$	$48 \div 4 = 12$	$96 \div 8 = 12$

Division facts related to the 3 times table	Division facts related to the 6 times table	Division facts related to the 12 times table
$3 \div 3 = 1$	$6 \div 6 = 1$	$12 \div 12 = 1$
$6 \div 3 = 2$	$12 \div 6 = 2$	$24 \div 12 = 2$
$9 \div 3 = 3$	$18 \div 6 = 3$	$36 \div 12 = 3$
$12 \div 3 = 4$	$24 \div 6 = 4$	$48 \div 12 = 4$
$15 \div 3 = 5$	$30 \div 6 = 5$	$60 \div 12 = 5$
$18 \div 3 = 6$	$36 \div 6 = 6$	$72 \div 12 = 6$
$21 \div 3 = 7$	$42 \div 6 = 7$	$84 \div 12 = 7$
$24 \div 3 = 8$	$48 \div 6 = 8$	$96 \div 12 = 8$
$27 \div 3 = 9$	$54 \div 6 = 9$	$108 \div 12 = 9$
$30 \div 3 = 10$	$60 \div 6 = 10$	$120 \div 12 = 10$
$33 \div 3 = 11$	$66 \div 6 = 11$	$132 \div 12 = 11$
$36 \div 3 = 12$	$72 \div 6 = 12$	$144 \div 12 = 12$

Division facts related to the 5 times table

$5 \div 5 = 1$

$10 \div 5 = 2$

$15 \div 5 = 3$

$20 \div 5 = 4$

$25 \div 5 = 5$

$30 \div 5 = 6$

$35 \div 5 = 7$

$40 \div 5 = 8$

$45 \div 5 = 9$

$50 \div 5 = 10$

$55 \div 5 = 11$

$60 \div 5 = 12$

Division facts related to the 10 times table

$10 \div 10 = 1$

$20 \div 10 = 2$

$30 \div 10 = 3$

$40 \div 10 = 4$

$50 \div 10 = 5$

$60 \div 10 = 6$

$70 \div 10 = 7$

$80 \div 10 = 8$

$90 \div 10 = 9$

$100 \div 10 = 10$

$110 \div 10 = 11$

$120 \div 10 = 12$

Fluency in Number Facts

Division facts related to the 7 times table	Division facts related to the 9 times table	Division facts related to the 11 times table
$7 \div 7 = 1$	$9 \div 9 = 1$	$11 \div 11 = 1$
$14 \div 7 = 2$	$18 \div 9 = 2$	$22 \div 11 = 2$
$21 \div 7 = 3$	$27 \div 9 = 3$	$33 \div 11 = 3$
$28 \div 7 = 4$	$36 \div 9 = 4$	$44 \div 11 = 4$
$35 \div 7 = 5$	$45 \div 9 = 5$	$55 \div 11 = 5$
$42 \div 7 = 6$	$54 \div 9 = 6$	$66 \div 11 = 6$
$49 \div 7 = 7$	$63 \div 9 = 7$	$77 \div 11 = 7$
$56 \div 7 = 8$	$72 \div 9 = 8$	$88 \div 11 = 8$
$63 \div 7 = 9$	$81 \div 9 = 9$	$99 \div 11 = 9$
$70 \div 7 = 10$	$90 \div 9 = 10$	$110 \div 11 = 10$
$77 \div 7 = 11$	$99 \div 9 = 11$	$121 \div 11 = 11$
$84 \div 7 = 12$	$108 \div 9 = 12$	$132 \div 11 = 12$

Multiples up to 12 × 12

Multiples of 2

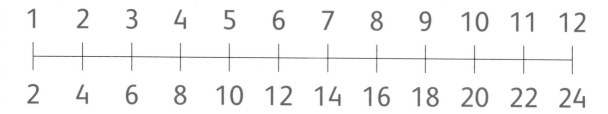

Multiples of 4

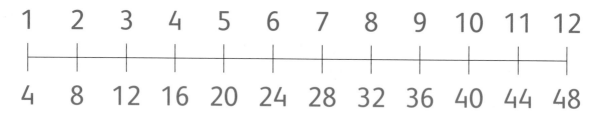

Multiples of 8

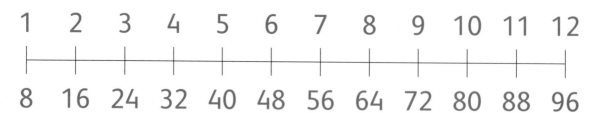

Fluency in Number Facts

Multiples of 3

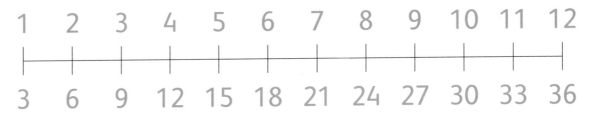

Multiples of 6

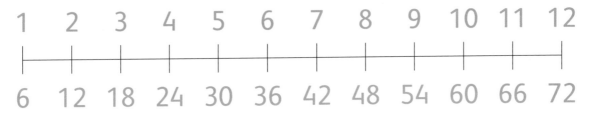

Multiples of 12

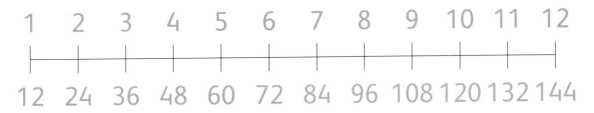

Multiples of 5

1	2	3	4	5	6	7	8	9	10	11	12
5	10	15	20	25	30	35	40	45	50	55	60

Multiples of 10

1	2	3	4	5	6	7	8	9	10	11	12
10	20	30	40	50	60	70	80	90	100	110	120

Multiples of 7

1	2	3	4	5	6	7	8	9	10	11	12
7	14	21	28	35	42	49	56	63	70	77	84

Multiples of 9

1	2	3	4	5	6	7	8	9	10	11	12
9	18	27	36	45	54	63	72	81	90	99	108

Multiples of 11

1	2	3	4	5	6	7	8	9	10	11	12
11	22	33	44	55	66	77	88	99	110	121	132

Fluency in Number Facts

Multiplication square to 12 × 12

×	2	3	4	5	6	7	8	9	10	11	12
1	1×2	1×3	1×4	1×5	1×6	1×7	1×8	1×9	1×10	1×11	1×12
2	2×2	2×3	2×4	2×5	2×6	2×7	2×8	2×9	2×10	2×11	2×12
3	3×2	3×3	3×4	3×5	3×6	3×7	3×8	3×9	3×10	3×11	3×12
4	4×2	4×3	4×4	4×5	4×6	4×7	4×8	4×9	4×10	4×11	4×12
5	5×2	5×3	5×4	5×5	5×6	5×7	5×8	5×9	5×10	5×11	5×12
6	6×2	6×3	6×4	6×5	6×6	6×7	6×8	6×9	6×10	6×11	6×12
7	7×2	7×3	7×4	7×5	7×6	7×7	7×8	7×9	7×10	7×11	7×12
8	8×2	8×3	8×4	8×5	8×6	8×7	8×8	8×9	8×10	8×11	8×12
9	9×2	9×3	9×4	9×5	9×6	9×7	9×8	9×9	9×10	9×11	9×12
10	10×2	10×3	10×4	10×5	10×6	10×7	10×8	10×9	10×10	10×11	10×12
11	11×2	11×3	11×4	11×5	11×6	11×7	11×8	11×9	11×10	11×11	11×12
12	12×2	12×3	12×4	12×5	12×6	12×7	12×8	12×9	12×10	12×11	12×12

×	2	3	4	5	6	7	8	9	10	11	12
1	2	3	4	5	6	7	8	9	10	11	12
2	4	6	8	10	12	14	16	18	20	22	24
3	6	9	12	15	18	21	24	27	30	33	36
4	8	12	16	20	24	28	32	36	40	44	48
5	10	15	20	25	30	35	40	45	50	55	60
6	12	18	24	30	36	42	48	54	60	66	72
7	14	21	28	35	42	49	56	63	70	77	84
8	16	24	32	40	48	56	64	72	80	88	96
9	18	27	36	45	54	63	72	81	90	99	108
10	20	30	40	50	60	70	80	90	100	110	120
11	22	33	44	55	66	77	88	99	110	121	132
12	24	36	48	60	72	84	96	108	120	132	144

Fluency in Number Facts

Trios for the multiplication tables to 12 × 12

2 times table and related division facts

$1 \times 2 = 2$
$2 \times 1 = 2$
$2 \div 2 = 1$
$2 \div 1 = 2$

Triangle: 2, 1, 2

$2 \times 2 = 4$
$4 \div 2 = 2$

Triangle: 4, 2, 2

$3 \times 2 = 6$
$2 \times 3 = 6$
$6 \div 2 = 3$
$6 \div 3 = 2$

Triangle: 6, 3, 2

$4 \times 2 = 8$
$2 \times 4 = 8$
$8 \div 2 = 4$
$8 \div 4 = 2$

Triangle: 8, 4, 2

$5 \times 2 = 10$
$2 \times 5 = 10$
$10 \div 2 = 5$
$10 \div 5 = 2$

Triangle: 10, 5, 2

$6 \times 2 = 12$
$2 \times 6 = 12$
$12 \div 2 = 6$
$12 \div 6 = 2$

Triangle: 12, 6, 2

$7 \times 2 = 14$
$2 \times 7 = 14$
$14 \div 2 = 7$
$14 \div 7 = 2$

Triangle: 14, 7, 2

$8 \times 2 = 16$
$2 \times 8 = 16$
$16 \div 2 = 8$
$16 \div 8 = 2$

Triangle: 16, 8, 2

$9 \times 2 = 18$
$2 \times 9 = 18$
$18 \div 2 = 9$
$18 \div 9 = 2$

Triangle: 18, 9, 2

$10 \times 2 = 20$
$2 \times 10 = 20$
$20 \div 2 = 10$
$20 \div 10 = 2$

Triangle: 20, 10, 2

$11 \times 2 = 22$
$2 \times 11 = 22$
$22 \div 2 = 11$
$22 \div 11 = 2$

Triangle: 22, 11, 2

$12 \times 2 = 24$
$2 \times 12 = 24$
$24 \div 2 = 12$
$24 \div 12 = 2$

Triangle: 24, 12, 2

3 times table and related division facts

$1 \times 3 = 3$
$3 \times 1 = 3$
$3 \div 3 = 1$
$3 \div 1 = 3$

$2 \times 3 = 6$
$3 \times 2 = 6$
$6 \div 3 = 2$
$6 \div 2 = 3$

$3 \times 3 = 9$
$9 \div 3 = 3$

$4 \times 3 = 12$
$3 \times 4 = 12$
$12 \div 3 = 4$
$12 \div 4 = 3$

$5 \times 3 = 15$
$3 \times 5 = 15$
$15 \div 3 = 5$
$15 \div 5 = 3$

$6 \times 3 = 18$
$3 \times 6 = 18$
$18 \div 3 = 6$
$18 \div 6 = 3$

$7 \times 3 = 21$
$3 \times 7 = 21$
$21 \div 3 = 7$
$21 \div 7 = 3$

$8 \times 3 = 24$
$3 \times 8 = 24$
$24 \div 3 = 8$
$24 \div 8 = 3$

$9 \times 3 = 27$
$3 \times 9 = 27$
$27 \div 3 = 9$
$27 \div 9 = 3$

$10 \times 3 = 30$
$3 \times 10 = 30$
$30 \div 3 = 10$
$30 \div 10 = 3$

$11 \times 3 = 33$
$3 \times 11 = 33$
$33 \div 3 = 11$
$33 \div 11 = 3$

$12 \times 3 = 36$
$3 \times 12 = 36$
$36 \div 3 = 12$
$36 \div 12 = 3$

4 times table and related division facts

$1 \times 4 = 4$
$4 \times 1 = 4$
$4 \div 4 = 1$
$4 \div 1 = 4$

4

1   4

$2 \times 4 = 8$
$4 \times 2 = 8$
$8 \div 4 = 2$
$8 \div 2 = 4$

8

2   4

$3 \times 4 = 12$
$4 \times 3 = 12$
$12 \div 4 = 3$
$12 \div 3 = 4$

12

3   4

$4 \times 4 = 16$
$16 \div 4 = 4$

16

4   4

$5 \times 4 = 20$
$4 \times 5 = 20$
$20 \div 4 = 5$
$20 \div 5 = 4$

20

5   4

$6 \times 4 = 24$
$4 \times 6 = 24$
$24 \div 4 = 6$
$24 \div 6 = 4$

24

6   4

$7 \times 4 = 28$
$4 \times 7 = 28$
$28 \div 4 = 7$
$28 \div 7 = 4$

28

7   4

$8 \times 4 = 32$
$4 \times 8 = 32$
$32 \div 4 = 8$
$32 \div 8 = 4$

32

8   4

$9 \times 4 = 36$
$4 \times 9 = 36$
$36 \div 4 = 9$
$36 \div 9 = 4$

36

9   4

$10 \times 4 = 40$
$4 \times 10 = 40$
$40 \div 4 = 10$
$40 \div 10 = 4$

40

10   4

$11 \times 4 = 44$
$4 \times 11 = 44$
$44 \div 4 = 11$
$44 \div 11 = 4$

44

11   4

$12 \times 4 = 48$
$4 \times 12 = 48$
$48 \div 4 = 12$
$48 \div 12 = 4$

48

12   4

5 times table and related division facts

$1 \times 5 = 5$
$5 \times 1 = 5$
$5 \div 5 = 1$
$5 \div 1 = 5$

$2 \times 5 = 10$
$5 \times 2 = 10$
$10 \div 5 = 2$
$10 \div 2 = 5$

$3 \times 5 = 15$
$5 \times 3 = 15$
$15 \div 5 = 3$
$15 \div 3 = 5$

$4 \times 5 = 20$
$5 \times 4 = 20$
$20 \div 5 = 4$
$20 \div 4 = 5$

$5 \times 5 = 25$
$25 \div 5 = 5$

$6 \times 5 = 30$
$5 \times 6 = 30$
$30 \div 5 = 6$
$30 \div 6 = 5$

$7 \times 5 = 35$
$5 \times 7 = 35$
$35 \div 5 = 7$
$35 \div 7 = 5$

$8 \times 5 = 40$
$5 \times 8 = 40$
$40 \div 5 = 8$
$40 \div 8 = 5$

$9 \times 5 = 45$
$5 \times 9 = 45$
$45 \div 5 = 9$
$45 \div 9 = 5$

$10 \times 5 = 50$
$5 \times 10 = 50$
$50 \div 5 = 10$
$50 \div 10 = 5$

$11 \times 5 = 55$
$5 \times 11 = 55$
$55 \div 5 = 11$
$55 \div 11 = 5$

$12 \times 5 = 60$
$5 \times 12 = 60$
$60 \div 5 = 12$
$60 \div 12 = 5$

6 times table and related division facts

$1 \times 6 = 6$
$6 \times 1 = 6$
$6 \div 6 = 1$
$6 \div 1 = 6$

$2 \times 6 = 12$
$6 \times 2 = 12$
$12 \div 6 = 2$
$12 \div 2 = 6$

$3 \times 6 = 18$
$6 \times 3 = 18$
$18 \div 6 = 3$
$18 \div 3 = 6$

$4 \times 6 = 24$
$6 \times 4 = 24$
$24 \div 6 = 4$
$24 \div 4 = 6$

$5 \times 6 = 30$
$6 \times 5 = 30$
$30 \div 6 = 5$
$30 \div 5 = 6$

$6 \times 6 = 36$
$36 \div 6 = 6$

$7 \times 6 = 42$
$6 \times 7 = 42$
$42 \div 6 = 7$
$42 \div 7 = 6$

$8 \times 6 = 48$
$6 \times 8 = 48$
$48 \div 6 = 8$
$48 \div 8 = 6$

$9 \times 6 = 54$
$6 \times 9 = 54$
$54 \div 6 = 9$
$54 \div 9 = 6$

$10 \times 6 = 60$
$6 \times 10 = 60$
$60 \div 6 = 10$
$60 \div 10 = 6$

$11 \times 6 = 66$
$6 \times 11 = 66$
$66 \div 6 = 11$
$66 \div 11 = 6$

$12 \times 6 = 72$
$6 \times 12 = 72$
$72 \div 6 = 12$
$72 \div 12 = 6$

7 times table and related division facts

$1 \times 7 = 7$
$7 \times 1 = 7$
$7 \div 7 = 1$
$7 \div 1 = 7$

$2 \times 7 = 14$
$7 \times 2 = 14$
$14 \div 7 = 2$
$14 \div 2 = 7$

$3 \times 7 = 21$
$7 \times 3 = 21$
$21 \div 7 = 3$
$21 \div 3 = 7$

$4 \times 7 = 28$
$7 \times 4 = 28$
$28 \div 7 = 4$
$28 \div 4 = 7$

$5 \times 7 = 35$
$7 \times 5 = 35$
$35 \div 7 = 5$
$35 \div 5 = 7$

$6 \times 7 = 42$
$7 \times 6 = 42$
$42 \div 7 = 6$
$42 \div 6 = 7$

$7 \times 7 = 49$
$49 \div 7 = 7$

$8 \times 7 = 56$
$7 \times 8 = 56$
$56 \div 7 = 8$
$56 \div 8 = 7$

$9 \times 7 = 63$
$7 \times 9 = 63$
$63 \div 7 = 9$
$63 \div 9 = 7$

$10 \times 7 = 70$
$7 \times 10 = 70$
$70 \div 7 = 10$
$70 \div 10 = 7$

$11 \times 7 = 77$
$7 \times 11 = 77$
$77 \div 7 = 11$
$77 \div 11 = 7$

$12 \times 7 = 84$
$7 \times 12 = 84$
$84 \div 7 = 12$
$84 \div 12 = 7$

Fluency in Number Facts

8 times table and related division facts

$1 \times 8 = 8$
$8 \times 1 = 8$
$8 \div 8 = 1$
$8 \div 1 = 8$

$2 \times 8 = 16$
$8 \times 2 = 16$
$16 \div 8 = 2$
$16 \div 2 = 8$

$3 \times 8 = 24$
$8 \times 3 = 24$
$24 \div 8 = 3$
$24 \div 3 = 8$

$4 \times 8 = 32$
$8 \times 4 = 32$
$32 \div 8 = 4$
$32 \div 4 = 8$

$5 \times 8 = 40$
$8 \times 5 = 40$
$40 \div 8 = 5$
$40 \div 5 = 8$

$6 \times 8 = 48$
$8 \times 6 = 48$
$48 \div 8 = 6$
$48 \div 6 = 8$

$7 \times 8 = 56$
$8 \times 7 = 56$
$56 \div 8 = 7$
$56 \div 7 = 8$

$8 \times 8 = 64$
$64 \div 8 = 8$

$9 \times 8 = 72$
$8 \times 9 = 72$
$72 \div 8 = 9$
$72 \div 9 = 8$

$10 \times 8 = 80$
$8 \times 10 = 80$
$80 \div 8 = 10$
$80 \div 10 = 8$

$11 \times 8 = 88$
$8 \times 11 = 88$
$88 \div 8 = 11$
$88 \div 11 = 8$

$12 \times 8 = 96$
$8 \times 12 = 96$
$96 \div 8 = 12$
$96 \div 12 = 8$

9 times table and related division facts

$1 \times 9 = 9$
$9 \times 1 = 9$
$9 \div 9 = 1$
$9 \div 1 = 9$

$2 \times 9 = 18$
$9 \times 2 = 18$
$18 \div 9 = 2$
$18 \div 2 = 9$

$3 \times 9 = 27$
$9 \times 3 = 27$
$27 \div 9 = 3$
$27 \div 3 = 9$

$4 \times 9 = 36$
$9 \times 4 = 36$
$36 \div 9 = 4$
$36 \div 4 = 9$

$5 \times 9 = 45$
$9 \times 5 = 45$
$45 \div 9 = 5$
$45 \div 5 = 9$

$6 \times 9 = 54$
$9 \times 6 = 54$
$54 \div 9 = 6$
$54 \div 6 = 9$

$7 \times 9 = 63$
$9 \times 7 = 63$
$63 \div 9 = 7$
$63 \div 7 = 9$

$8 \times 9 = 72$
$9 \times 8 = 72$
$72 \div 9 = 8$
$72 \div 8 = 9$

$9 \times 9 = 81$
$81 \div 9 = 9$

$10 \times 9 = 90$
$9 \times 10 = 90$
$90 \div 9 = 10$
$90 \div 10 = 9$

$11 \times 9 = 99$
$9 \times 11 = 99$
$99 \div 9 = 11$
$99 \div 11 = 9$

$12 \times 9 = 108$
$9 \times 12 = 108$
$108 \div 9 = 12$
$108 \div 12 = 9$

Fluency in Number Facts

10 times table and related division facts

$1 \times 10 = 10$
$10 \times 1 = 10$
$10 \div 10 = 1$
$10 \div 1 = 10$

10 / 1 10

$2 \times 10 = 20$
$10 \times 2 = 20$
$20 \div 10 = 2$
$20 \div 2 = 10$

20 / 2 10

$3 \times 10 = 30$
$10 \times 3 = 30$
$30 \div 10 = 3$
$30 \div 3 = 10$

30 / 3 10

$4 \times 10 = 40$
$10 \times 4 = 40$
$40 \div 10 = 4$
$40 \div 4 = 10$

40 / 4 10

$5 \times 10 = 50$
$10 \times 5 = 50$
$50 \div 10 = 5$
$50 \div 5 = 10$

50 / 5 10

$6 \times 10 = 60$
$10 \times 6 = 60$
$60 \div 10 = 6$
$60 \div 6 = 10$

60 / 6 10

$7 \times 10 = 70$
$10 \times 7 = 70$
$70 \div 10 = 7$
$70 \div 7 = 10$

70 / 7 10

$8 \times 10 = 80$
$10 \times 8 = 80$
$80 \div 10 = 8$
$80 \div 8 = 10$

80 / 8 10

$9 \times 10 = 90$
$10 \times 9 = 90$
$90 \div 10 = 9$
$90 \div 9 = 10$

90 / 9 10

$10 \times 10 = 100$
$100 \div 10 = 10$

100 / 10 10

$11 \times 10 = 110$
$10 \times 11 = 110$
$110 \div 10 = 11$
$110 \div 11 = 10$

110 / 11 10

$12 \times 10 = 120$
$10 \times 12 = 120$
$120 \div 10 = 12$
$120 \div 12 = 10$

120 / 12 10

11 times table and related division facts

$1 \times 11 = 11$
$11 \times 1 = 11$
$11 \div 11 = 1$
$11 \div 1 = 11$

$2 \times 11 = 22$
$11 \times 2 = 22$
$22 \div 11 = 2$
$22 \div 2 = 11$

$3 \times 11 = 33$
$11 \times 3 = 33$
$33 \div 11 = 3$
$33 \div 3 = 11$

$4 \times 11 = 44$
$11 \times 4 = 44$
$44 \div 11 = 4$
$44 \div 4 = 11$

$5 \times 11 = 55$
$11 \times 5 = 55$
$55 \div 11 = 5$
$55 \div 5 = 11$

$6 \times 11 = 66$
$11 \times 6 = 66$
$66 \div 11 = 6$
$66 \div 6 = 11$

$7 \times 11 = 77$
$11 \times 7 = 77$
$77 \div 11 = 7$
$77 \div 7 = 11$

$8 \times 11 = 88$
$11 \times 8 = 88$
$88 \div 11 = 8$
$88 \div 8 = 11$

$9 \times 11 = 99$
$11 \times 9 = 99$
$99 \div 11 = 9$
$99 \div 9 = 11$

$10 \times 11 = 110$
$11 \times 10 = 110$
$110 \div 11 = 10$
$110 \div 10 = 11$

$11 \times 11 = 121$
$121 \div 11 = 11$

$12 \times 11 = 132$
$11 \times 12 = 132$
$132 \div 11 = 12$
$132 \div 12 = 11$

12 times table and related division facts

$1 \times 12 = 12$
$12 \times 1 = 12$
$12 \div 12 = 1$
$12 \div 1 = 12$

△ 12 / 1 12

$2 \times 12 = 24$
$12 \times 2 = 24$
$24 \div 12 = 2$
$24 \div 2 = 12$

△ 24 / 2 12

$3 \times 12 = 36$
$12 \times 3 = 36$
$36 \div 12 = 3$
$36 \div 3 = 12$

△ 36 / 3 12

$4 \times 12 = 48$
$12 \times 4 = 48$
$48 \div 12 = 4$
$48 \div 4 = 12$

△ 48 / 4 12

$5 \times 12 = 60$
$12 \times 5 = 60$
$60 \div 12 = 5$
$60 \div 5 = 12$

△ 60 / 5 12

$6 \times 12 = 72$
$12 \times 6 = 72$
$72 \div 12 = 6$
$72 \div 6 = 12$

△ 72 / 6 12

$7 \times 12 = 84$
$12 \times 7 = 84$
$84 \div 12 = 7$
$84 \div 7 = 12$

△ 84 / 7 12

$8 \times 12 = 96$
$12 \times 8 = 96$
$96 \div 12 = 8$
$96 \div 8 = 12$

△ 96 / 8 12

$9 \times 12 = 108$
$12 \times 9 = 108$
$108 \div 12 = 9$
$108 \div 9 = 12$

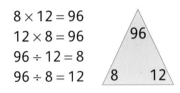

△ 108 / 9 12

$10 \times 12 = 120$
$12 \times 10 = 120$
$120 \div 12 = 10$
$120 \div 10 = 12$

△ 120 / 10 12

$11 \times 12 = 132$
$12 \times 11 = 132$
$132 \div 12 = 11$
$132 \div 11 = 12$

△ 132 / 11 12

$12 \times 12 = 144$
$144 \div 12 = 12$

△ 144 / 12 12

Recognise the place value of each digit in a 3-digit number (hundreds, tens and ones) and a 4-digit number (thousands, hundreds, tens and ones)

Lucky 7
A game for 2 players

You need:
- pencil and paperclip (for the spinner)
- about 12 counters

Before you start:
- Decide whether you are going to use the purple spinner and building (for 3-digit numbers) or the green spinner and building (for 4-digit numbers).

Take turns to:
- spin the spinner
- work out the place value of the 7
- place a counter on one of the matching place values on the building.

Golden rule
- If all the matching place values are covered, miss that turn.

The winner is:
- the first player to complete a line of 4 counters. A line can go sideways ←→, up and down ↕, or diagonally ↘.

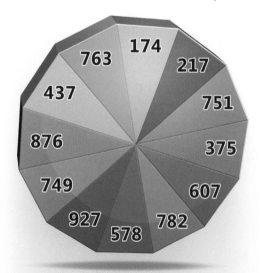

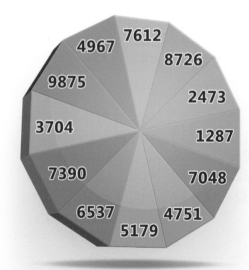

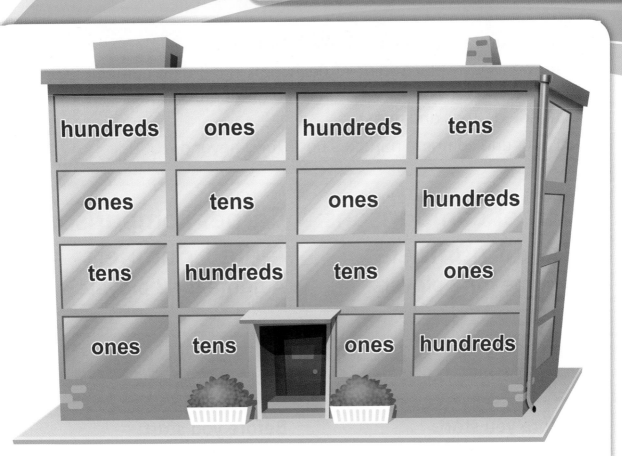

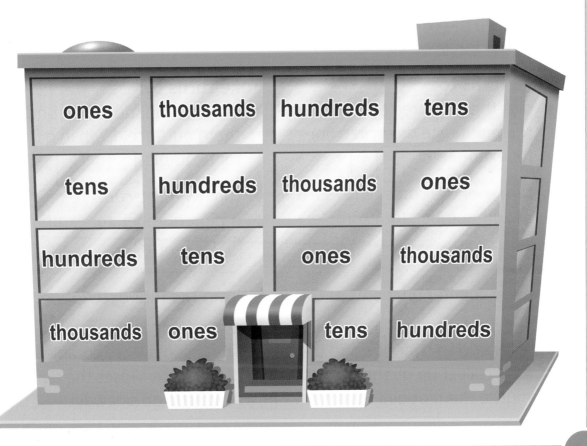

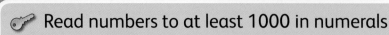

🔑 Read numbers to at least 1000 in numerals

🔑 Recognise the place value of each digit in a 3-digit number (hundreds, tens and ones) and a 4-digit number (thousands, hundreds, tens and ones)

🔑 Order and compare numbers up to, and beyond, 1000

Carpet comparisons: 3-digit numbers
A game for 2 players

Carpet comparisons: 4-digit numbers
A game for 2 players

You need:
- set of 1–9 number cards
- about 20 counters

Before you start:
- Use the purple carpet.

Before you start:
- Use the green carpet.

- Shuffle the cards and place them face down in a pile in the middle of the table.

Take turns to:
- pick the top three cards and lay them out face down in a line, for example: ▢▢▢

Take turns to:
- pick the top four cards and lay them out face down in a line, for example: ▢▢▢▢

- turn over the cards to reveal a 3-digit number, for example:

6 2 1

- turn over the cards to reveal a 4-digit number, for example:

4 1 7 5

- put a counter on a part of the carpet that fits that description.

Golden rule
- After each player has had a turn, collect up all the cards and shuffle them again.

How to win:
- The first player to complete a line of 3 counters **loses** the game. A line can go sideways ↔, up and down ↕, or diagonally ↘.

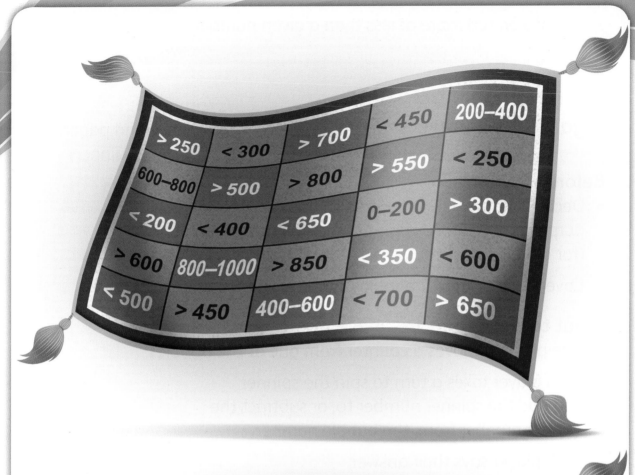

			< 450	200–400
> 250	< 300	> 700	> 550	< 250
600–800	> 500	> 800	0–200	> 300
< 200	< 400	< 650	< 350	< 600
> 600	800–1000	> 850	< 700	> 650
< 500	> 450	400–600		

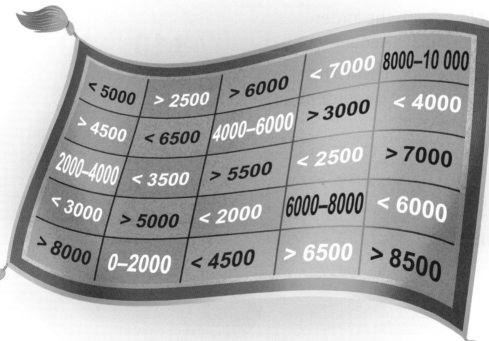

			< 7000	8000–10 000
< 5000	> 2500	> 6000	> 3000	< 4000
> 4500	< 6500	4000–6000	< 2500	> 7000
2000–4000	< 3500	> 5500	6000–8000	< 6000
< 3000	> 5000	< 2000	> 6500	> 8500
> 8000	0–2000	< 4500		

🔑 Find 10 or 100 more or less than a given number

More or less bubbles
A game for 2 players

You need:
- pencil and paperclip (for the spinner)
- 12 counters

Before you start:
- Decide whether you are going to use the purple bubbles (for 3-digit numbers) or the green bubbles (for 4-digit numbers).
- Cover each of the 12 bubble numbers with a counter.

What to do:
- One player removes a counter from one of the bubbles.
- Each player takes a turn to spin the spinner and add the spinner number to, or subtract the spinner number from, the bubble number.
- Each player says their answer.
- The player with the larger answer keeps the counter.
- Repeat the above with the other player removing a counter from one of the bubbles.
- Continue until all 12 counters have been removed from the bubbles.

The winner is:
- the player with more counters.

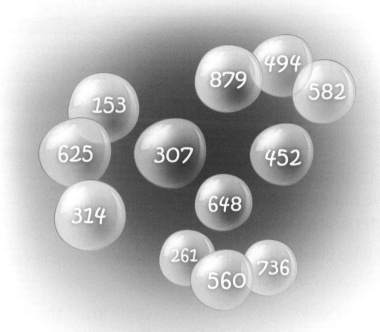

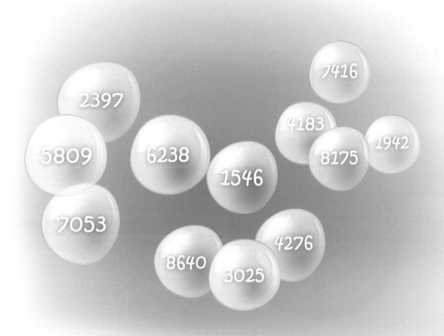

Count in multiples of 2, 3, 4, 5, 10, 50 and 100

And the winner is...
A game for 2 players

You need:
- pencil and paperclip (for the spinners)
- 10 counters

What to do:
- Take turns to choose a spinner. Spin the spinner. The number you spin is the winning number. Put a counter on this number to remind you.
- The player who chose and spun the spinner starts the count from the 'Starting from...' number.
- Take turns to 'count on in...' or 'count back in...' the steps shown. (For example, Player A says: '2', Player B says '4', Player A says '6' etc. until the winning number is reached.)
- The winner is the player who says the number with the counter on it. They take the counter.
- Play 10 rounds.

The winner is:
- the player with more counters.

Starting from 2, count on in 2s

Starting from 3, count on in 3s

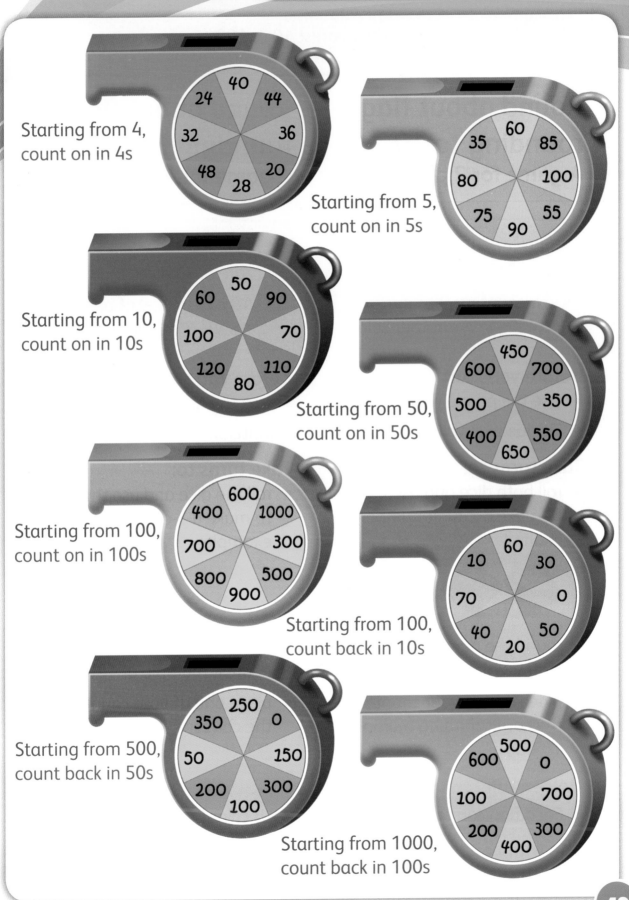

Starting from 4, count on in 4s

40 · 44 · 36 · 20 · 28 · 48 · 32 · 24

Starting from 5, count on in 5s

60 · 85 · 100 · 55 · 90 · 75 · 80 · 35

Starting from 10, count on in 10s

50 · 90 · 70 · 110 · 80 · 120 · 100 · 60

Starting from 50, count on in 50s

450 · 700 · 350 · 550 · 650 · 400 · 500 · 600

Starting from 100, count on in 100s

600 · 1000 · 300 · 500 · 900 · 800 · 700 · 400

Starting from 100, count back in 10s

60 · 30 · 0 · 50 · 20 · 40 · 70 · 10

Starting from 500, count back in 50s

250 · 0 · 150 · 300 · 100 · 200 · 50 · 350

Starting from 1000, count back in 100s

500 · 0 · 700 · 300 · 400 · 200 · 100 · 600

🔑 Round any number to the nearest 10 or 100

Round about flags: rounding to 10
A game for 2 players

You need:
- two 0–9 dice
- 18 counters: 9 of one colour, 9 of another colour

Before you start:
- Use the purple flags.
- Decide who will have which colour counters.

Take turns to:
- roll both dice and use the digits to make a 2-digit number, for example:

 95 or 59

- round the number to the nearest multiple of 10
- place one of your counters on the corresponding multiple of 10 flag.

Round about flags: rounding to 100
A game for 2 players

You need:
- three 0–9 dice
- 18 counters: 9 of one colour, 9 of another colour

Before you start:
- Use the green flags.

Take turns to:
- roll the dice and use the digits to make a 3-digit number, for example:

 598, 958...

- round the number to the nearest multiple of 100
- place one of your counters on the corresponding multiple of 100 flag.

Golden rule
- Each flag can take one counter of each colour.

The winner is:
- the first player to put their counters on 9 different flags.

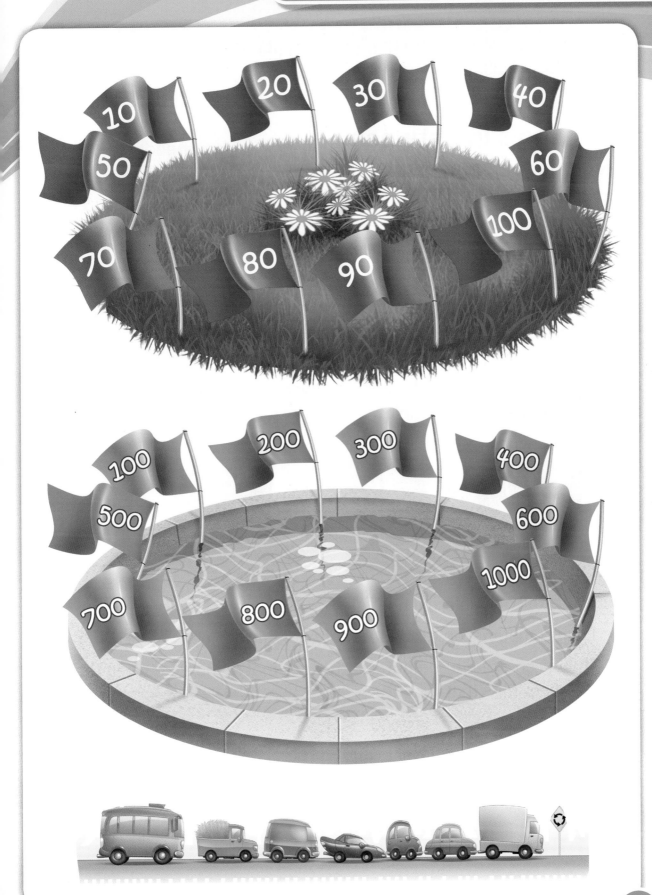

🔑 Compare numbers with the same number of decimal places up to two decimal places

Decimals in between
A game for 2 players

You need:
- two 1–6 dice
- 30 counters: 15 of one colour, 15 of another colour

Before you start:
- Decide who will have which colour counters.

Take turns to:
- roll both dice, for example:
- place one of your counters on any computer which shows a decimal number between the dice numbers, for example:

 or  or

Golden rules
- If you roll a double, roll both dice again.
- Each computer can take one counter of each colour.
- If you can't find a computer with a decimal number between the dice numbers, miss that turn.

The winner is:
- the first player to put their counters on 15 different computers.

Add and subtract mentally two 2-digit multiples of 10

Button up
A game for 2 players

You need:
- pencil and paperclip (for the spinner)
- 24 counters

Before you start:
- Decide who will cover the blue buttons and who will cover the orange buttons.

Take turns to:
- spin the spinner twice
- add the two numbers together, say the answer and cover that button
- find the difference between the two numbers, say the answer and cover that button.

Golden rule
- If the button beside one, or both, of the answers is already covered, you cannot cover it with another counter.

The winner is:
- the first player to place 12 counters on their buttons.

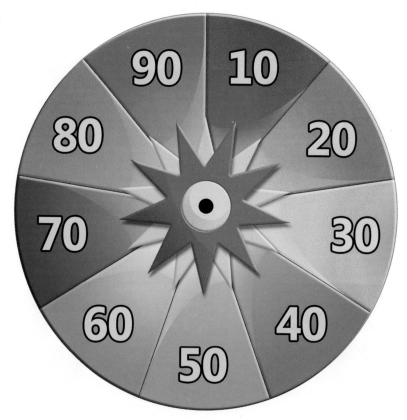

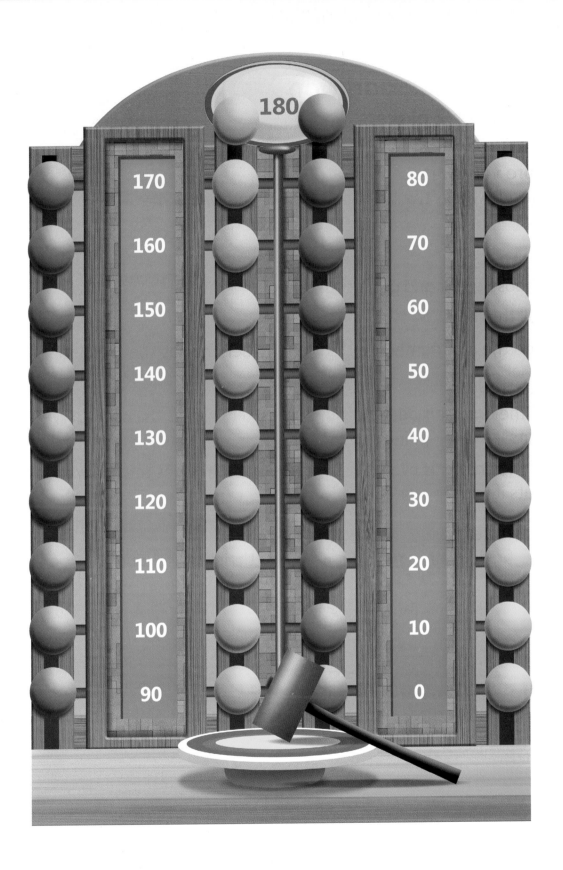

Add and subtract mentally a 2-digit number and ones

Star catcher: addition
A game for 2 players

You need:
- 0–9 dice
- 20 counters

Before you start:
- Decide who is the Odd Star Catcher and who is the Even Star Catcher.

Take turns to:
- choose a star and put a counter on it
- roll the dice
- add the dice number to the star number and say the calculation.

> Be sure not to cover up the number.

Golden rules
- If the answer is odd, the Odd Star Catcher takes the counter and puts it in their pair of hands.
- If the answer is even, the Even Star Catcher takes the counter and puts it in their pair of hands.

The winner is:
- the first player to put 10 counters in their pair of hands.

Variation:

Star catcher: subtraction
- Subtract the dice number from the star number and say the calculation.

Odd Star Catcher

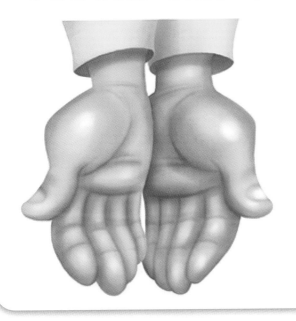

Even Star Catcher

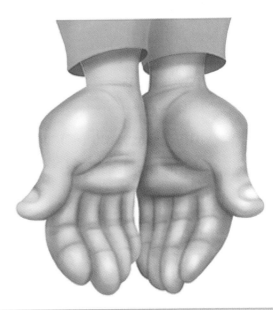

Fluency in Number Facts

🔑 Add and subtract mentally two 2-digit numbers

The coin decides: addition
A game for 2 players

The coin decides: subtraction
A game for 2 players

You need:
- 24 counters
- coin

Before you start:
- Cover each of the numbers on the notice board with a counter.

What to do:
- Each player removes two counters from the notice board and adds their two numbers together.

What to do:
- Each player removes two counters from the notice board and works out the difference between their two numbers.

- When players have shared their answers, one player tosses the coin.

Golden rules

Heads

Tails

Larger answer wins

Smaller answer wins

- The winner keeps all 4 counters removed from the notice board.
- Keep going until all 24 counters have been removed from the notice board.

The winner is:
- the player with more counters.

Add and subtract mentally a 3-digit number and ones

The Ferris wheel: addition
A game for 2 players

You need:
- button
- two 0–9 dice: 1 for each player
- 20 counters

What to do:
- Place the button on any child on the Ferris wheel.
- One player rolls their dice and moves the button that number of cabins around the Ferris wheel.
- Each player then rolls their dice and adds the dice number to the number on the cabin.
- Players share their calculations.
- The player with the larger answer takes a counter.
- Continuing moving around the Ferris wheel, alternating who rolls the dice to move the button on.

Golden rule
- If you roll a zero, roll the dice again.

The winner is:
- the first player to collect 10 counters.

Variation:

The Ferris wheel: subtraction
- Each player rolls their dice and subtracts the dice number from the number on the cabin. The player with the smaller answer takes a counter.

Add and subtract mentally 3-digit numbers and tens

Six cars wins
A game for 2 players

You need:
- 12 counters: 6 for each player
- button
- pencil and paperclip (for the spinner)

Before you start:
- Decide which spinner to use:

  Red spinner: adding 3-digit numbers and tens

  Blue spinner: subtracting 3-digit numbers and tens

  Green spinner: adding and subtracting 3-digit numbers and tens.

- Put the button on the .

Take turns to:
- move the button one step around the coloured steering wheels
- spin the spinner
- add or subtract the spinner number to or from the number with the button on it.

Golden rules
- If the answer is on one of the cars, cover it with one of your counters.
- If the answer is not on one of the cars, or is already covered by a counter, miss that turn.

The winner is:
- the first player to place all of their counters on any 6 cars.

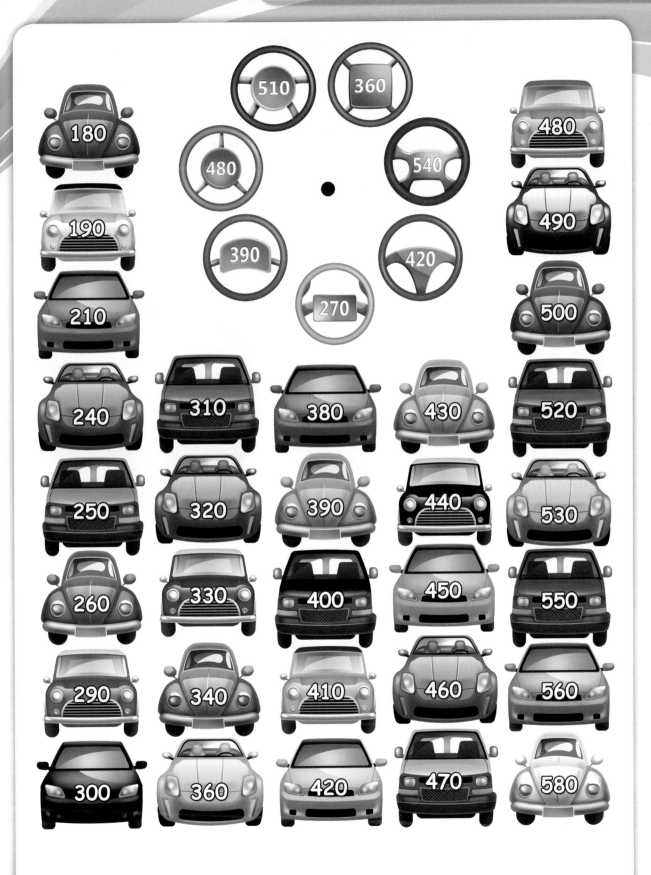

Fluency in Number Facts

Add and subtract mentally a 3-digit number and hundreds

Hit the target
A game for 2 players

You need:
- button
- pencil and paperclip (for the spinner)
- about 30 counters

Take turns to:
- put the button on a dart
- spin the spinner
- add or subtract the spinner number to or from the dart number and cover the answer on the target with a counter.

Golden rule
- If the answer is not on the dartboard, or is already covered by a counter, miss that turn.

The winner is:
- the first player to complete a row of 4 numbers in one of these ways:

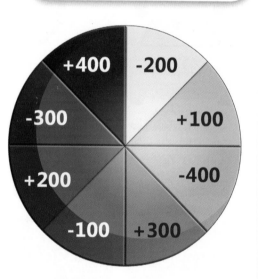

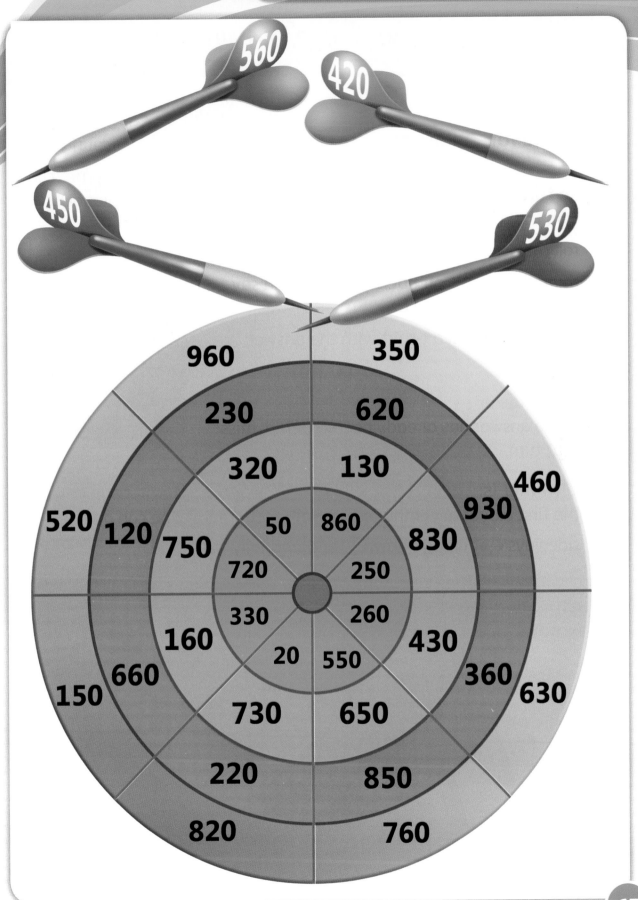

Recall multiplication facts for the 2, 5 and 10 multiplication tables

Team lines
A game for 2 players

You need:
- about 30 counters
- pencil and paperclip (for the spinner)
- 1–12 dice

Take turns to:
- spin the spinner
- roll the dice
- multiply the two numbers together and say the multiplication fact
- put a counter on a t-shirt with the answer on it.

Golden rule
- If the answer has already been covered, miss that turn.

The winner is:
- the first player to complete a line of 4 counters. A line can go sideways ↔, up and down ↕, or diagonally ↘.

Recall multiplication facts for the 3, 4 and 8 multiplication tables

3, 4 and 8 cube
A game for 2 players

You need:
- 1–12 dice
- about 30 counters

Take turns to:
- roll the dice
- decide whether to multiply the dice number by 3, 4 or 8
- say the calculation
- cover the answer on the cube.

Golden rule
- If the answer has already been covered, miss that turn.
- If the answer is not on the cube, miss that turn.

The winner is:
- the first player to complete a line of 6 numbers over two faces of the cube, for example:

× 3

or

× 4

or

× 8

Recall multiplication facts for the 6, 7, 9, 11 and 12 multiplication tables

Win the world
A game for 2 players

Before you start:
- Decide who will have which colour counters.

You need:
- 24 counters: 12 of one colour, 12 of another colour
- 1–12 dice

× 6

or

× 7

or

× 9

or

× 11

or

× 12

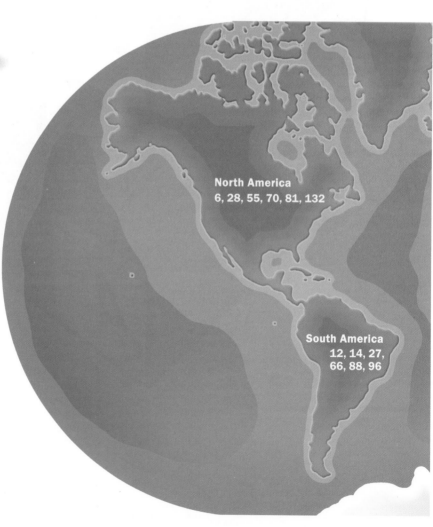

North America
6, 28, 55, 70, 81, 132

South America
12, 14, 27, 66, 88, 96

Take turns to:

- roll the dice

- decide whether to multiply the dice number by 6, 7, 9, 11 or 12

- say the calculation

- put a counter on the continent that has that number.

Continue until all 24 counters have been placed on the map.

The player with more counters on a continent controls that continent. If both players have the same number of counters on a continent, that continent stays neutral – no one wins it!

The winner is:

- the player who controls the most continents.

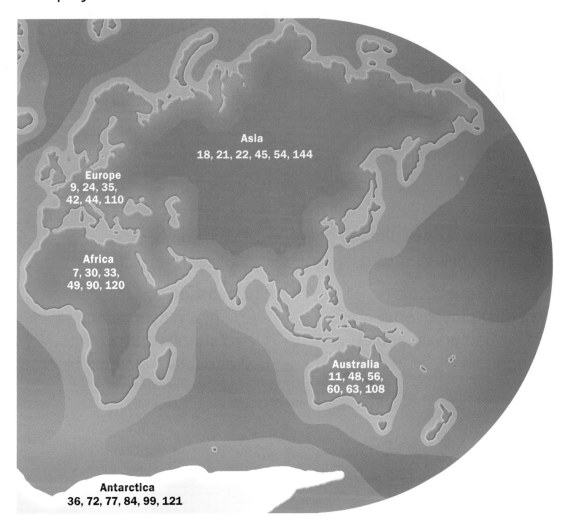

Asia
18, 21, 22, 45, 54, 144

Europe
9, 24, 35,
42, 44, 110

Africa
7, 30, 33,
49, 90, 120

Australia
11, 48, 56,
60, 63, 108

Antarctica
36, 72, 77, 84, 99, 121

Recall multiplication and division facts for multiplication tables up to 12×12

Honeycomb: multiplication
A game for 2 players

You need:
- two 1–12 dice
- about 30 counters

Take turns to:
- roll both dice
- multiply the two numbers together and say the multiplication fact
- cover the answer on the honeycomb.

Golden rule
- If the answer has already been covered, miss that turn.

The winner is:
- the first player complete a line of 4 numbers up and down ↕, diagonally ↖↘ or in a block:

Honeycomb: division
A game for 2 players

You need:
- 1–12 dice
- about 30 counters

Take turns to:
- roll the dice
- find a multiple of the number rolled on the honeycomb and say the division fact
- cover the number.

Golden rule
- If you can't find a multiple of the number spun, miss that turn.

The winner is:
- the first player complete a line of 7 numbers up and down ↕, diagonally ↖↘ or in a block:

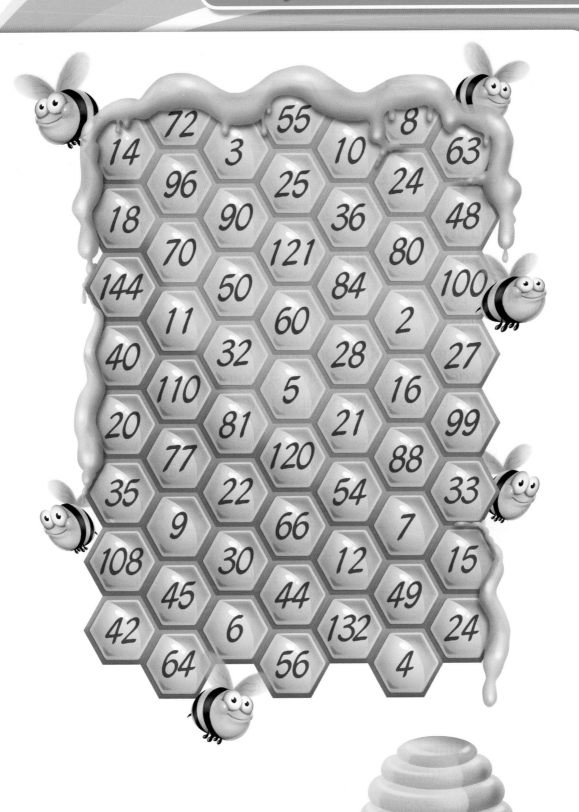

Recall multiplication and division facts for multiplication tables up to 12×12

River times
A game for 2 players

You need:
- 1–12 dice
- 9 counters

Before you start:
- Place a counter on each child.

Take turns to:
- roll the dice
- move **1** of the 9 counters forward 1 step if the next number on the stepping stone is a multiple of the number rolled, for example:

60 is a multiple of 12

60   22   36   63   9   64

Golden rules
- You can only move 1 counter each turn.
- If you can't move a counter, miss that turn.

How to win:
- When a counter reaches the stone on the other side of the river, the player who moved the counter takes the counter.
- The first player to collect 3 counters is the overall winner.

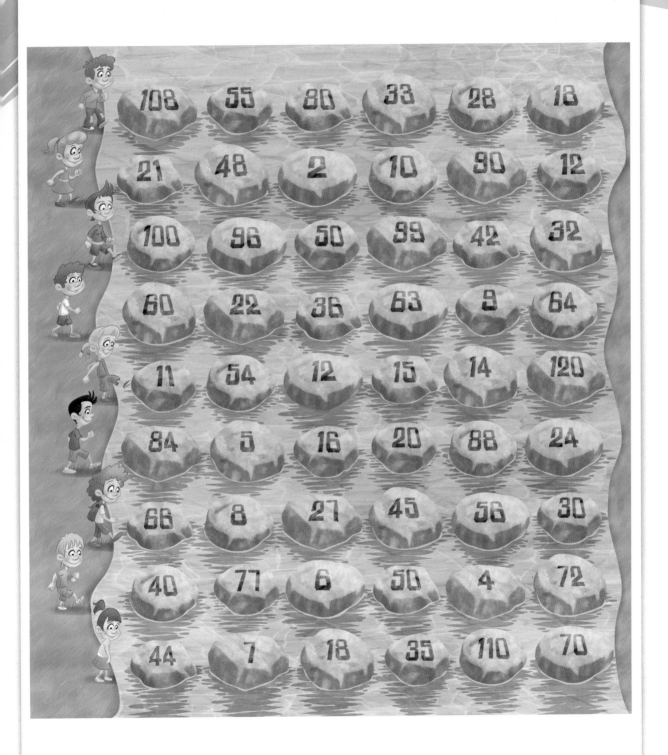

Multiply a 2-digit number by a 1-digit number

Mechanical multiplication
A game for 2 players

You need:
- button
- two 1–6 dice: 1 for each player
- 8 counters: 4 for each player
- pencil and paper (optional)

What to do:
- Place the button on any cog of the machine.
- One player rolls their dice and moves the button that number of cogs around the machine.
- Each player then rolls their dice and multiplies their dice number by the cog number.
- Players share their calculations.
- If the answer is one of the box numbers, place a counter on that box.
- Repeat the above with the other player rolling their dice and moving the button that number of cogs around the machine.

YOU CAN USE PENCIL AND PAPER TO HELP YOU WORK OUT THE ANSWER.

Golden rules
- If you roll a 1, roll the dice again.
- Each box can only have 1 counter on it.

The winner is:
- the first player to put their 4 counters on the boxes.

Calculate mathematical statements for division using known multiplication tables

Hunting Yeti
A game for 2 players

Before you start:
- Decide who will have which colour counter.
- Place the counters at Base Camp.

Take turns to:
- spin the spinner
- roll the dice
- divide the spinner number by the dice number
- say the calculation
- move your counter forward the number of footprints of the remainder, for example:

You need:
- 2 counters of different colours
- pencil and paperclip (for the spinner)
- 1–6 dice

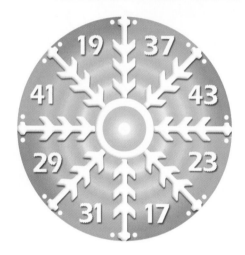

23 divided by 5 is 4 remainder 3. I can move my counter on 3 footprints.

Golden rule
- If you roll a 1, roll the dice again.

The winner is:
- the first player to reach Yeti.

Base Camp

Fluency in Number Facts

Resources used in *Fluency in Number Facts* Years 3 & 4

Key domain	Game	Pages	counters	1–9 number cards	pencil and paperclip (for the spinner)	1–6 dice	0–9 dice	1–12 dice	button	coin	pencil and paper
Number and place value	Lucky 7	42–43	•		•						
	Carpet comparisons	44–45	•	•							
	More or less bubbles	46–47	•		•						
	And the winner is…	48–49	•		•						
	Round about flags	50–51	•				•				
	Decimals in between	52–53	•			•					
Addition and subtraction	Button up	54–55	•		•						
	Star catcher	56–57	•				•				
	The coin decides	58–59	•							•	
	The Ferris wheel	60–61	•				•		•		
	Six cars wins	62–63	•		•				•		
	Hit the target	64–65	•		•				•		
Multiplication and division	Team lines	66–67	•		•			•			
	3, 4 and 8 cube	68–69	•					•			
	Win the world	70–71	•					•			
	Honeycomb	72–73	•					•			
	River times	74–75	•					•			
	Mechanical multiplication	76–77	•				•			•	•
	Hunting Yeti	78–79	•		•		•				

How to use a spinner

Some of the paired games in this book require a spinner. This is easily made using a pencil, a paperclip and the spinner printed on each games page. Hold the paperclip in the centre of the spinner using the pencil and gently flick the paperclip with your finger to make it spin.